Reflections of a Woman's Heart

Dear Florence,
 I love you! Thank you for being a wonderful friend and neighbor! God Bless you!
    Love Always
    Tammy A Kemper

Reflections of a Woman's Heart

A Journey

Poetry and Psalms by
Tammy A. Kemper

Copyright © 2011 by Tammy A. Kemper.

Library of Congress Control Number: 2011905104
ISBN: Hardcover   978-1-4568-9793-2
                Softcover   978-1-4568-9792-5
                Ebook   978-1-4568-9794-9

All rights reserved. No part of this book may be reproduced or transmitted in any form or by any means, electronic or mechanical, including photocopying, recording, or by any information storage and retrieval system, without permission in writing from the copyright owner.

This book was printed in the United States of America.

To order additional copies of this book, contact:
Xlibris Corporation
1-888-795-4274
www.Xlibris.com
Orders@Xlibris.com
96784

Contents

Introduction 9

The Heart of My Journey 11

    The Journey 13
    Mirrors 14
    The Child Inside 16
    The Capture 17
    My Name 18
    It Will Come 19

The Heart of Praise 21

    Adoni 23
    The Psalms of Calming 24
    The Prism 25
    Draw Me Close Today 26
    Song of Praise 27
    Psalms of Groaning 29
    Why Lord? 30
    My Broken Heart 31
    Faithful to the Cause 32
    The Two Adams 33

The Heart of my Uniqueness 35

    Lord, the Value of Me 37
    Thank You, Lord 38
    A Humble Spirit 39
    Springs of Water 40
    Changing Me 41

- Colors 42
- Reflections 43
- Constraints and Roles 44
- Intense 45
- Ponderance 46
- Vanities 47
- Cross Roads 48

The Heart of Relationships 49

- The Heart of Family 51
- To My Paula 52
- To My Tamara 53
- To My son Stephen 54
- My grandbabies 55
- My Second Grandchild 57
- Remembrance of Mary 58
- Amazing Love 59
- A Eulogy of Love 60
- The Heart of Love 61
- Right and Wrong 62
- Behave 63
- The Story of Tamar 64
- Guardian Angel 65
- Awakenings 66
- Bittersweet Desire 67
- The Heart of Friendship 68
- The Charmer 69
- Gentle Plea 70

The Heart of Nature 73

- Gentle Showers 75
- Storms of Life 76
- Beautiful Spring 78
- Snapshot of a View 79
- Soaring Free 80

Dedication

I want to dedicate this book to all my friends and family. Paula Wray you are such a wonderful person. Your praise and encouragement gave me such inspiration to fulfill my dreams of writing my first book. Paula, my sweet daughter, you say I am your hero, but sweetie you are mine. Thanks to my wonderful son, Stephen, who helped me so much with putting my work in manuscript form. Thanks to my husband for sharing my dreams. John your beautiful music and friendship has inspired me so much. Cara thank you for being my friend and loving me as I am. Elana thank you so much for your help and for a new friendship! I love you all.

Introduction

Approximately a year and a half ago, I embarked on a beautiful journey to become the woman that I longed to be, overcoming a lifetime of food addiction and low self-esteem. With the help of my heavenly Father, friends, and family I found the inspiration to put together my first book. Although I have written poetry and Psalms for many years I never had the courage, until now, to share it with other people. Every poem I have written, good or bad, reflects how I feel about my Savior, personal relationships, and the world around me. My prayer is that if I can help just one person through my experiences then it will be a true blessing.

I am very grateful and humbled by those who have been a support system in my life. The wonderful ladies of Curves have been a true support system as well as some of my closest friends. I am so humbled by their love and encouragement as I am finally living the dreams that I have dreamed.

A special "Thank you" for all the doctors who have helped me realize my dream of losing over 100 pounds. I have more to go, but I am inspired to see it to the goal I have set. You all have truly saved my life. Thank you for never giving up on me. I am fortunate to have had the "dream team" of doctors who have helped me overcome my medical problems and achieve a healthier lifestyle.

I want to thank my wonderful church family, who has been a great source of encouragement to me as well. Your love and feedback on my poetry has meant so much to me. You are the family that has loved me through so much and been a godly inspiration in all I do. All the scriptures that I have put with my poems have been taken from the King James Version of the Bible.

My journey is not over! There is so much more to discover. There are fantastic things that make up the uniqueness of me, a rich full life until my time on earth is over. I am excited to share with others the reflections of my heart. The journey I am on to become the beautiful woman on the outside to reflect the beautiful woman I have always been on the inside.

The Heart of My Journey

This is my journey. It is a journey that started long before I even became aware of my very being. As with the Ancient ones of old, the Lord is with me every step of the way. This is a story of Christ's love for me as I have learned to love myself, a written expression of the highs and lows of self-discovery of the last year and a half. Thank You, Lord, for my journey, a journey that continues till my time on earth ends.

The Journey

As I think back over time I realize how far I've come.
Fantastic things have come my way born out of great sorrow and pain.
The Valleys I've traveled have been very low,
But the mountaintops are so supremely divine making me feel so alive.

I raise my arms to my Lord as I enjoy the glorious highs of his love.
But when troubles do descend; I must remember to praise Him even then.
An offering of Thanksgiving I give for the blessings I behold.
Praise to the lover of my soul who makes me complete and whole.

Thank You, Father, for being next to me
And for sometimes carrying me when I was too weak.
Help me to remember You are always my strength!
Yes Lord, this is my journey that defines the uniqueness that is mine.
Until it comes to an end let me always live this life more fully.

2010

I Thessalonians 5:18 In everything give thanks; for this is the will of God in Christ Jesus concerning you.

Mirrors

As I behold the reflections of my soul,
What do I see?
Do I see the actual face staring back at me?

Often I behold the perceptions of what a woman should be.
Do I seek unrealistic ideas of beauty?

As I look through the mirrors of my mind,
I often find distortions of reality
Of what is actually on the outside.

My fragile self-image is marred
By the deceptions of air-brushed imagery
Offered up for sale.

Lord, I often buy into such things.
Led astray by the misconceptions,
By the world of vain perfections.

It grieves me to hear any woman say,
"I'm not good enough,"
Not measuring up to such societal standards.

I understand these things,
Because mirrored back to me
Is the obscured image of what true beauty should be.

Teach me Lord what truly is.
Nothing You create is ugly or bad.
In You exists true worth.

I am a beautiful woman inside and out,
Made in Your glorious image
To reflect Your gems of fine qualities.

Encourage me Lord to see
That loveliness comes from having your heart
Of tenderness and the face of forgiveness.

Let me explore the values of a virtuous woman
And see the truth mirrored
Through the eyes of God.

2010

Proverbs 31:30 . . . but a woman who fears the Lord shall be praised.

The Child Inside

There stands a young child who gazes at the distant hills and horizons.
As her tortured soul awaits and dreams of places of contentment.
She longs for escapes of bliss far from her desperate fate.
As she overlooks fields of grassy knolls with pristine blue skies for miles,
With soft warm breezes.
Yes, her spirit is confined which longs to glide past great sorrow and brokenness.
And we are left to ponder what awaits this sweet child beckoned to roam so far away.

Where did she go, this child?
Did she get lost or did she find her way?
Or did she get covered up somewhere along the way?
Like a caterpillar who spins its cocoon.
She's hidden by those trials that have her entombed.
Longing to be empowered and to escape the wrappings that bind.
Inside a need to evolve before she awakes.

As the transformation takes place, strength returns
As slowly the child inside is sculpted to be truly unique.
As the layers come off, the spiritual and physical both converge
To show the true loveliness that laid dormant so long.
This colorful butterfly will emerge to flutter high above
To be wrapped instead in the wondrous colors of the wind and sun.
Surrounded by the flowers of life
Having survived tumultuous rainstorms throughout the long night.
But it is this that brings the growth of abounding love
And brings about seasons of supreme rebirth.

Psalms 121:1,2 I will look up mine eyes unto the hills, from whence cometh my help. My help cometh from the Lord, which made heaven and earth.

The Capture

Did you know you have captured this wild and lonely heart?
Unlocking the inner sanctuary of my painful and private thoughts.
Giving me the courage and freedom
To embrace the things that make up the very core and being of my faith,
The things I live and walk through most every day.

Your patience and kindness has reigned me in.
Thus I explore with bravery all of my artistic fears
Bringing to life the things held way down deep inside my very being.

Your words and thoughts flow through me,
Capturing within my mind the way I feel.
Sparking within me you, a most kindred spirit.

I am humbled and touched by your praise.
Happy and blessed that you love the things
That have come directly from the very essence of how I think.

Many years I wrote about the things upon my heart.
Too scared to show my words.
Never thinking what I wrote was good enough or thinking others would care.

But God has brought into my life those who have inspired
And given me hope that my words have great worth.
An inspiration to share.

I am thankful for this talent that my Lord has given to me.
The capturing of my heart is the written expression of joy
That is a part of my life most every day.

2010

Proverbs 18:24 A man that hath friends must shew himself friendly; there is a friend that sticketh closer than a brother.

My Name

I am a graceful palm tree full of grace
Hebrew words full of faith
You are the God of my name
Fearfully and wonderfully made
A conception of truth!

I am a woman Lord, full of faults.
But your blood covers and sanctifies my heart.
Nothing can be hid
You know my deepest and darkest fears.

Convictions whispered by the spirit pricks my very soul
As I struggle with life's unfairness
And those who would choose to have a name of sin and worldly pleasures.

Help me Lord to choose to be pure and humble
Not knowing why evil happens
Acknowledging Lord You are in control of things I cannot fathom.

Lord, thank You for my name
A beautiful, delightful gift that lets me know that
You are with me all the way as I walk the narrow path to your heavenly gates.

August 10, 2010

Isaiah 45:4 . . . I have called you by your name. I have named you.

It Will Come

Day by day I am working hard learning to be more patient.
My confidence is making me secure as I gain understanding.

My abilities are growing stronger as I'm learning to love myself.
I'm taking more in stride as I learn to live and laugh.

I hold in my heart a secret.
I'm just waiting when all can be put to right with a new revelation.
A tantalizing living hope!

The dedication to the hard work will be rewarded.
The prize I gain will be a life changing experiences.

But until then I will believe in myself despite what others think.
I will become the beautiful spirit that longs to be free.

When the time is perfect and I'm at my best,
Things will come together.
My hope and dreams will be fulfilled at last!

2010

Romans 8:23 But if we hope for that we see not, then do we with patience wait for it.

The Heart of Praise

Oh let my heart always praise You my Lord; whether it be in happiness or sadness. As I journey on I have found it easier to understand why it is necessary to praise God in all things. King David in Psalms always came to the Lord honestly in all situations he found himself in. He was able to praise God in the good times as well as the times that brought him to the depth of despair. God loves us and wants us to come to Him with our thankfulness as well as our complaints. So as I walk more closely with my heavenly Father, I find it natural to praise Him in all things. It is what draws me and keeps me close to Him. Praising Him is as natural to me as the air I breathe.

Adoní

Heavenly Father I've fallen in love with You all over again.
You are my first love; the beginning and the end. The great I AM.
Oh Adoni, let me praise You and give thanks for keeping me safe
And bringing me back once again to Your Holy place.

Your mercies are renewed with each new day.
Your grace is long-suffering and Your patience's knows no date.
You answer my prayers in perfect timing and in Your own way
Seeing the whole picture, knowing what's best for the day.

As a child, Lord, sometimes I'm stubborn and impatient,
But You always know how to humble me with Your loving presence.
You are my supreme power, who loves me as I am.
You cover me with tenderness, and in Your loving care I have no fear.

You are the Lord most high. Let me have no shame.
Telling others of Your salvation and living each day in divine faith.
Fortune and fame I could seek; but Lord nothing I see compares
To the riches that are waiting for me.

Let my exhortations be of Your unending goodness.
So others will know that You are the true God of all creation!
Adoni, let me praise You continuously.
Prostrate before You as I strive to be a living sacrifice all of my days!

2010

Joel 2:27 . . . I Am the Lord Your God and there is no other . . . .

The Psalms of Calming

Lord, down on my knees
I've come to bring to You all my wants and needs.
Sharing with You my most intimate and private cares and pain.

As I pray and meditate on Your heavenly realm,
Let me delight in your refreshing love
That brings calmness and healing for my weary and broken heart.

Forgive me Lord and bring me back to rest in your holiness.
Bring this soul so restless to abide in Your gentleness.
Lead me to paths of Your righteousness.

Lay me down to rest in Your loving arms
And give me peace of a thousand years of eternal bliss.
The cool still waters that run through the valley of unrest.

Take away from me these earthly fears and burdens.
Letting go of the worries of such worldly things.
Giving to me instead Your loving and carefree spirit.

Lord You are my Shepard; my soul longs for you.
Guide and direct my life with the gentle rod of your loving ways
Interlaced with great wisdom and grace.

Let me always dwell in Your house of praise.
Let my cup overflow with thankfulness.
To live my life serving You all the rest of my days.

2010

Psalms 23:1 The Lord is my Shepard I shall not want.

The Prism

Seeing God and His reflections,
I come to see the desires that reveal the true colors of my heart.
Do I reflect Your holy thoughts or the craziness of my deceitful and sinful heart?

Do I share the news of amazing grace?
Shining forth your holiness of your wonderful face.
The kaleidoscope of unending hope and faith.

Clean up my heart, Lord, so I can show others
The brightness of your agape love.
And then I can stand before You
A temple that is used for Your service above.

Lord, let me reflect Your godliness
Shown forth by shades of brilliant faith.
Seeing His reflections, I come back to see
That He has always been my first true love.

Gently remind me, Lord, that You are the cornerstone of my life
Anchored and secured through Your unending grace.
Freeing my heart to always be Yours.
I am Your ambassador to reflect your gift of salvation given to our earthly shores.
A beacon of Your sacrifice for all who would desire eternal life.

The Lord is the lighthouse of my heart.
Sheltering me from the storms of life.
Always there to light my way.
Delighting in the prism of Your wonderful love.

2010

Psalms 51:10 Create in me a clean heart and renew a right spirit within me.

Draw Me Close Today

Draw me close, Lord.
Wrap me in your arms.
Tame this wild and unruly heart.
And keep me from wandering afar.

Sketch into my soul the artistry of Your word.
Help me to understand the holiness of Your loving thoughts.
Shape and mold me into all I could be.

With the guidance of the Holy Spirit,
Who breathes life into my very being.
As I kneel at the cross of Your Salvation,
Thank You Jesus for embracing me
With all the blessings of Your love.
Then in turn let me be an encouragement to those I meet.
Who also hurt and need Your loving touch.

Let my faith never waiver
As I am learning to depend on You.
Giving me courage as I walk through all these changes.

Thank You Lord for lifting me up from this worldly depression.
Showing me Your gloriousness and a far better existence.
Let my works reflect forth the righteousness and gentleness
Of Your spirit shown through this earthen vessel.
Extolling with humbleness a witness of Your greatness
With each encounter You send through the day.

Draw me close Lord.
Seek me in the morning.
Let me walk with You through the evening
Before falling asleep in Your loving embracement.

2010

Psalms 73:28 For it is good to draw near to God. I have put my trust in the Lord God. That I may declare all Your Works.

Song of Praise

Lord, I am so grateful for Your healing touch.
Thank You for covering me with Your grace.
Giving me a strong healthy heart full of faith.

With every heartbeat remind me, Lord,
To take care of this temple that is Yours.
Fill it with Your holiness and Your never-ending love.

Thank You Lord for giving me a clean heart.
I am humbled that You have touched me
With Your powerful healing touch!

Remind me to serve You each and every day.
Remembering how far You have brought me in this journey
For You have carried me most of the way.

Oh Holy Spirit fill this vessel and bring to me
Your sweet, sweet yearning to always worship and serve my Savior.
Being always grateful to One who loves me!

Baptize me in your fiery presence.
Set my heart afire, to never tire in my journey
As I strive to always be Yours.
Speaking in my soul Your beautiful language.

With my tongue let me always sing and speak Your praise.
Showing to others Your virtues and goodness
Being thankful for Your answer to my prayers.

Thank You Lord, for faithful friends
Who prayed lifting me up before Your throne
And for those who took care of me guided by Your loving arms.

Fill me Lord with Your humility as I travel on.
Give me strength;
Renew my soul and spirit with Your supernatural love sent from above.

2010

Psalms 22:23 Ye that fear the Lord, praise him . . . glorify him; and fear him . . . .

Psalms of Groaning

Thank You Lord for giving to me such joy and peace.
The trials I'm walking are so hurtful, raw and deep.
I am sure that You see what will be a better place of relief.
Plans to prosper and make me complete.
You give me no harm.
Loving discipline makes me strong.
A need to be refined in the wine press of love.
I cry, Oh Abba Father!
You are my rock and my salvation.
Loosening my tongue to praise the wonders of Your loving face!
Walk me Lord through this adversity and pain.
My very soul imprinted and engraved on the palms of Your loving hands of grace.
I leave to You those who are so wicked and insane.
Things that cause me to groan and writhe in agony and pain.
Take away this root of bitterness.
Cut it out of me.
Let me be as a strong, sturdy tree bearing sweet fruits of truth.
Ingrain in me the need to stand firm,
Planted and rooted in life-giving waters.
Steadfast to never waiver in Your love and favor.

August 10, 2010

Psalms 6:6 I am weary with my groaning; all the night make I my bed to swim; I water my couch with my tears.

Why Lord?

Lord, why do I let the wicked get inside my mind?
My heart cries when I am hurt by such desires.
There are things in my life that are so unfair.
I am stuck in a place I don't really want to live.
Such things make me want to scream.

But yet I must be calm for those around me would judge me most unworthy.
These things test me sorely; I only want to be free.
Get away from the wickedness and those who want to use me.
Lord take away these snares and the troubles I see.
Fill my life with hope and the glory that could be.

Please take from me this discouragement that is a plague.
Send instead, encouragement to help me live.
Some around me are so into themselves.
They are so shallow they think only of themselves; there's no substance!

Lord, I want so much more.
I'm seeking and searching for answers to the things I don't understand.
Often I question why did You even create man?
Finding real love and kindness is something that is very rare.

But one thing I know is that the pleasures of this world are not for me.
Only blessings and love through You truly exist.
I need you Lord every day; day by day I must live.
It is only through Christ I must find my very existence.

2010

Psalms 37:10 For yet a little while, and the wicked shall not be: yea, thou shalt diligently consider his place, and it shall not be.

My Broken Heart

Psalms 147:3 He heals the brokenhearted and binds up their wounds.

Help me Lord through this time.
The unknown makes me anxious.
Take this fear and let me hide in your loving places.
Take this heart that is broken and hear my pleas for Your healing.
You Lord, are the great physician!
The supreme power as my heart is beating.

You, oh God, are my friend.
The lover who satisfies my soul.
My praises are for You alone
Because in comparison there is no other.

I will extol you!
My mighty redeemer!
Let me bow and praise You as the angels above.
Lift me up to see Your court of glory,
On the soft wings of a peaceful dove.

Lord, take my heart and fix it.
Clean it up with Your love.
Wash and make it worthy.
Touched by the powerful fingers of Your healing touch!

Faithful to the Cause

We must rejoice for the future.
Do not cry for the past.
Live for the Lord in this present day because God's spirit is among us at last.

Hear our cry, Oh Lord;
Bring to us Your kingdom, a new heaven and earth.
Help us persevere and be faithful in Your heavenly work.

God will shake the heavens
And the nations will bow down
And all will acknowledge on bended knees that He is the great I AM!

God will bring us together.
Our works will be tried and purified with His holy fire.
We will worship in His omnipotent presence and giving praise to Him will be our desire.

Help us Lord!
Fill us with Your holy spirit.
Give us endurance to fight so that the victorious glory of the cross can be shown to the lost and dying world.

Do not tire oh Christian Soldier.
Be faithful to the cause.
We must endure to the end because the victory is His and Satan will never win!

2010

Philipians 2:10 That at the name of Jesus every knee shall bow, of things in heaven, and things in earth and things under the earth.

The Two Adams

As the first Adam came from dust; the second came from heaven.
One fell into sin and the other came to save us.
Temptation was too great for man,
So, our Savior came to earth to bring us hope of eternal love
And the gift of Salvation.
On Calvary Jesus died; the sacrificial lamb.
To bring about the spiritual rebirth
To bridge the path between God and Man.
The Holy Spirit convicts the heart and waits for our response.
It is our choice to repent and turn from our wicked thoughts.
Then will God forgive our sins and give us healing and peace,
Accepting His free gift in Jesus, we only have to believe.
So today, my friend, what you will do?
Will you deny Him or choose to be spiritually reborn
Closing the gap between the two.

2010

Romans 10:9,10 That if thou shalt confess with thy mouth the Lord Jesus, and shalt believe in thine heart that God hath raised him from the dead, thou shalt be saved. For with the heart man believeth unto righteousness; and with the mouth confession is made unto salvation.

The Heart of my Uniqueness

You knew me before I even drew my first breathe. I am fearfully and wonderfully made in Your image. In this journey I discover daily who I am as I walk the narrow path. Thank You, Lord, for revealing Yourself as I grow and mature in Your love and grace. Thank You for the wonderful things that make me truly unique! Let me, Lord, always with humility, be the beautiful woman You created on the inside as well as the outside.

Lord, the Value of Me

You Lord, love me as I am.
Where others condemn; You never treat me with disdain or let me down.
There are days I feel no one cares,
That I am nothing in compare.
My heart often aches with this despair.

I know You gave me these feelings and emotions.
But they seem to take a toll;
Especially when they become the focus.
These things make me feel naked and bare,
Which leads me to wonder who I really am.

Teach me Lord, not to worry.
Show me Your valuable lessons from above
And the wonderful mercy's of Your unconditional love.

2010

Romans 8:1 There is therefore no condemnation to them which are in Christ Jesus, who walk not after the flesh, but after the spirit.

Thank You, Lord

Thank you Lord for not judging me and caring whenever I am bad.
You forgive and never reject me and never deem me unworthy to be your friend.
Thank for not ignoring me and making me feel sad.
I am thankful that you never treat me like a child
And tell me to reflect on the things I have done and said.

Thank you for burying my sins in the deepest seas
And for not holding them against me.
It would be nice if others could reflect on their own sins
Instead of making judgments on me.
But I guess I realize that maybe if that is the way it is
It is probably better to stay away from such things
And be with those who really care and help me in my journey.
Help me Lord to be a better person.
To be softer and kinder.

Help me with the pain that is coming out
And send me people who will be a blessing.
I'm hurting Lord and trying to get a grip.
I'm doing the best I can.
But I am taking it a day at a time and I know
I will be a better person when things are said and done.

2010

Psalms 103:12 As far as the East is from the West; so far hath he removed our transgressions from us.

A Humble Spirit

Sometimes Lord, I feel foolish with pride.
Watch me stumble and fall in a blink of an eye.

Sometimes I feel happy and free then other times in deep misery.
Then will I fall on my knees.

Help me Lord not to be in vain
Judging and condemning others when I am often the blame.

Teach me tender love and care, holiness, and compassion for others
When I see them in despair.

Take away this selfishness I feel, of wanting it to be about me.
When it's really all about you!

Renew in me a sacrifice of praise.
Create within me a clean heart and humble spirit of faith.

2010

I Peter 5:5 . . . God resists the proud, but gives gace to the humble.

Springs of Water

Do I satisfy my soul at Your springs of water?
Or do I wander looking for such earthly wonders?

Do I quench the Holy Spirit as He whispers flowing messages that say,
Dwell here and be satisfied.
Don't stray away.

Lord, I'm like the woman at the well, who searched in vain.
Longing to fulfill her life with fleeting earthly gains.

And like her, You come to me, offering your eternal grace,
Unconditional and fulfilling deep waters of hope and faith.

Remind me Lord, every day, that Your springs of water
Are far better than all the worldly pleasures that I could ever partake.

2010

Psalms 16:11 . . . at thy right hand there are pleasures forever more.

Changing Me

Why be sad? What gives you such power in my life?
It's not you that gives me my gifts.
But it was you that brought inspiration back to life.

Why be so cruel? Is it a game?
I don't see what you have to gain. Am I yours to tame?
What is the great allure? A pleasure to see me broken?

The only One who has the right to break me and mold into His heart,
Loves me unconditionally and laid down His own life.
The supreme sacrifice. Are you willing to pay this price?

So don't tell me not to over think because it is my right as a human being.
From my mind come great things since I have this great capacity.
Why not be an encourager?

I'm an artist with great emotions.
My potential to love knows no bounds, and in my soul there is
The struggle to control the opposite side that can be so profound.

The One I bow down to everyday, is the only One
Who has the right to demand such things.
My heavenly Father in His gentle care molds me like a potter at his wheel.

He's shaping me and refining my very being.
He's the supreme artist of my very soul.
So relax, the job of changing me doesn't belong to you or anyone else!

2010

Isaiah 64:8 But now O Lord, Thou art our Father; we are the clay, and Thou art the Potter and we are the work of Thy hand.

Colors

I used to see my world in bright colors.
Purple, orange and glorious yellows.
Green, red and blue and all in a swirling neon motion.
Bursting sunrises in the morning sky
And the lingering soft glow of the sunset in the eventide.
The beautiful shades of the covenant rainbow
After the heart thumping thunderstorm pass by.

Yet sadly life brings sorrowing hues of black and white
Of grays that intermingles into a different haze.
But yet my dreams are of the colors of my younger days.

Sometimes you are the color of my mind.
Bright hues that are so sublime.
This makes me think of sparkling colors swirling me up to the heavens.
And then you hurt me with your words and then my colors aren't so bold.
Grays and blacks color my heart with dark purples
And violets deeply lower into my saddened soul.

This is how it is with me.
When happy, I see the world with the spectrum of colors high above
Or the darks of the underworld when I am really sad.

2010

Reflections

I saw an old lady today.
She was lovely in every way.
She was nicely dressed with every hair in place.
As I smile at her and she reciprocates,
I think what secrets lay behind her face?
What was her fate?
What was her life; was it fair?
Was it full of tender love and care?
Or did she encounter heart aches and snares?
Maybe it was a mixture of both,
But seeing her gives me hope that if I live to be that old
Maybe I will be her in that repose.

2010

Constraints and Roles

My mind is in such dizzying array!
I'm trying hard to behave.
I have these roles I must play and perform most every day.
But my heart tells me I want more.
I want to stray and explore.
I want to scream "don't box me in".
Don't ignore me; I'm still here!
I want someone to understand the frustrations that plague me in every way.
It's like opening Pandora's Box.
It won't stop and go away!
I want to stop these crazy things.
Which is worse?
Nothing or the haunting of these passions that put me in such pain?

Am I your audience to adore from far?
When I wish only to talk to you about what's mostly on my heart.
But Alas, I must be restrained
In these constraints and play the roles in which I am contained,
Just to be ignored.
But maybe I will seek another way to be released.
Surprising those around me who expect me to act in a certain way!
Can you guess what it could be?

2010

Intense

Why do I live like this?
Like an onion take my skin and peel it off!
I cannot go on like this! It feels too intense.

I want to live life full of passion
And shed the layers that have held me down
For what seems like forever.

Set me free!
I want to scream, I am me!
Love me and let me be the feelings I have that are down deep inside.

I am tired of having no passion in my life.
People tell me act your age and behave.
Day after day I go on doing the dutiful and mundane.

I am tired of it; I want out.
I want happiness, love and desire.
I am totally more than this.
Others see me and think she's so happy,
But inside I feel I'm dying.

I am trying to live; don't tell me to be proper.
I want to break free to walk on water.
I want to love, laugh and shed these restraints.
Let me go and let me OUT!!

2009

Ponderance

I was born in crisis.
Where do I find my place?
Sometimes I feel people can be so plastic and fake.
Am I facing it with boldness?
Where is my strength?
Especially, when I feel some are compassionless and blase.

What do I do with this?
Do I fight or hide?
Yes sometimes I want to just pack my bags and run far away.

Why can't people be honest?
Why is it so hard for some realization
Of how they are being so self-absorbed?

I'm tired of being lied to and strung alone.
Its hurts my very being
And I just want to say "Come on just be honest"!

So as I am pressed beyond measure
And ponder my thoughts,
I try to see past it all and see some real hope.
Surely, I can find others who feel the same way.
Hopefully fine qualities are not out of date.

Good manners and kindness hopefully have not died.
Such as saying "please" and "thank you"
And calling a friend who is down.
As I think about these things I hope I can
find it in my heart to be an example
Of what I write and ponder about.

2010

Vanities

I just want to run and hide from such human pettiness and pride.
Of ones who think they're so grand
Giving advice of love slobbering in their own importance.
Take me away from these cold formal things
Of people who compete and complain of such vanities.
I hate this; I hate that.
Oh look I'm so fat! Why I'm just a size eight.
Then in turn I hear them say,
But gee; you would never hear me talk bad of another.
But yet they just uttered the biggest slanders of themselves.
Instead, give me a warm heart who loves things of substance.
Whose treasures belie contentment, hope,
And selflessness that encompass the milk of human kindness.

2010

Psalms 36:6 I have hated them that regard lying vanities; but I trust in the Lord.

Cross Roads

I'm at a crossroads in my life.
Longing to tear down the walls that have been a shelter
And trying to kick down the roles that have been assigned for me.

Some are trying to tell me what I should do.
Give it time; all will be fine.
But who gave them the right?
It vexes me to hear such unsolicited advice.

I know I have choices; I know right from wrong.
I just want to break with such familiar sight.
I want to live a more passionate life.

As I ask myself this question,
I want to know why I can't have both and it be okay.
It would sadden me to know I couldn't have it both ways.

Don't tell me I'm kicking against the societal roles.
No one should be tethered to a sad and lonely life.
I just want to live more passionately.

I would rather die than live thinking that
I should make everyone happy and
Forget what I need and want for myself.
It would be most hypocritical.

So I wish everyone could see that
The changes I'm making will determine what will be.
Grow with me or just please get out of my way.

Because there is one thing for sure,
I'm not going to be the same old person that everyone expects of me.
I have changed and more changes you will see.

2010

The Heart of Relationships

It is important that in this journey of life that we have the experiences of satisfying and long lasting relationships. I am thankful for my husband of almost 20 years. Our relationship has not always been easy, but it has been very rewarding. We have three wonderful children and so far 3 fantastic grandchildren. Included are poems that I have written about family who have passed on and have had a huge impact on my life as a Christian and the person I am today. Thank You, Lord, for my friends and family. Thank You heavenly Father for being my friend and the lover of my soul.

The Heart of Family

FAMILY CURSES

Ripped away so young.
Having no say in what's going on.
Confused and feeling so vulnerable and alone.
The drama in the grown-up world.
Oblivious to the child that is left to wonder, "What is going on"?
Torn away.
Sibling from Sibling.
Many a year goes by.
Here one day and there tomorrow.
Sent to another life.
Pain and sorrow pushed aside.
Adjusting to a different place.
But yet there was remembrance of her name and face.
He said, she said.
They each had their story.
But the innocent ones are left to bear the scars of the family curses.
Meeting again one by one.
At last a reunion.
Loved one, so brave, giving names to tangible faces.
Some held abreast their grudges.
While others drew close.
But the heart will choose where to stay no matter the grievance.
Friends and loves can be chosen, often they come and go.
But family is the one thing that mankind has absolutely no control.

2010

To My Paula

The day you were born I was so happy.
As you snuggled and slept close to my beating heart,
I thought; it was so worth it.

You were so beautiful and perfect.
A baby girl delivered to me by God's angels
That rainy early morning after such hard labor.

As you lay upon my breast and suckled,
I fell deeply in love and pondered this awesome thing
Of being called a mother.

Now as I look back, it seems like yesterday
That I held you in my arms and felt such love
For this precious gift that God gave me that wonderful day.

You have a baby girl now who's just as sweet as you.
And I know you realize how special she is
And will be through the years.

So cherish every moment because life is so short.
Because before you know it she will grow
To be a beautiful woman with dreams of her own.

We could only hope and pray
That she will be extremely blessed to have her own special bundle
Sent by angels from heaven itself.

2010

To My Tamara

The day you were born I was depressed,
Because your father was with someone else.
But I was happy to see my little monkey!

You were red and long and gave a loud cry
And I laughed and welcomed you with my arms opened wide.
You were the light of my life.

Even though I was sad at the time,
Your sweet little countenance always cheered my mind.
You always had a lovely smile.

As you grew older you were my wild child.
An out of control drummer who marched to a different beat!
Many times you vexed me!

But alas, with time you grew up to be a beautiful woman
With lovely fine qualities.
An eccentric sweet person sort of like me!

Now you have two babes that are precious as they can be.
A boy and a girl who I long to see.
Enjoy them my sweet daughter for times goes by
And someday you'll wake up and find that they are grown and have their own lives.

I pray God's blessings for the years to come
When they experience the joys and pains of having new life.

2010

To My son Stephen

God gave me a dream of what would be.
A gift that would bless my womb.
A promise that soon came true.

When you were born it was a joy.
The day was sunny and fair.
Family and friends were there rejoicing at the news.

You were my son I longed for
And the apple of your dad's eye.
The last little one to complete the blessings of my life.

Now you are a teenager who's always full of life.
Sometimes your mouth makes me cringe
But you're still quite alright.

You look so smart in uniform
And always make good grades.
All this despite learning problems along the way.

Someday, you'll make a great father
With babies of your own.
I pray for that special wife God has waiting just for you.

Enjoy the many blessings that God has for you,
Because life is fleeting;
Remember to live it free and more abundantly.

2010

My grandbabies

My grandbabies are so lovely.
They are the reward of my heart.
A boy and a girl, one fair and the other so dark.
They are the sweetness that I behold.
The spirit of wholesomeness that runs deep in my soul.
They are my story to be told.

Each a joy in their own way.
Happiness surrounding their births
Even though they live so far away.
A wondrous distraction to me.
Makes me feel so grand and nice.
Giving me a reason to live a healthy and better life.

Gabriel, my first grandchild.
So handsome and full of life.
His dark eyes sparkle with mischievousness just like a little sprite.
His laughter is a delight.
Full of lyrical musical notes.
So enduring and pleasing to hear.
He has such lovely curly hair.

Hollie, my third so far,
Is so sweet and fair.
Her face is angelic and she has such beautiful blonde hair.
Her dimples in her cheeks are just like mine.
Her countenance so brilliant full of light.
She just wins me over with her smile!

My grandbabies just melt my heart.
I love them more than anything of my own.
They add such wonderful color to my home.
And when it is time for them to be going
I will be sad and long for them
when they go back to their overseas home.
I'll count the days till they return.
Think of them from day to day
And what they are doing as they live and play.
As their father serves his country so far away.

2010

My Second Grandchild

You were my first granddaughter.
My sweet little Caydence.
Born far from home on an Air Force base.
Your proud daddy called to tell me you were here,
Born on a cold, snowy Texas morning.

And then next spring on a warm Easter weekend
I finally got to see you.
My sweet little baby bunny!
My heart glowed in love as I held you in my arms
And looked upon your lovely face.
A most beautiful baby!

You had curly gold hair just like your mama's.
I laughed and teased your dad because you had his little nose.
The family cheeks were very prominently displayed.
Fat and rosy within such a cute little face!

I long to see you more often.
I pray for you each day.
Perhaps soon you will get to move back here someday.

2010

Remembrance of Mary

A great woman of love and faith.
Who loved the Lord in many ways.
You opened your heart to me to be the mother I desperately needed.

A great love clicked between us from the first day we met.
Never forsaking me.
Always there to help even as I suffered in the darkest and deepest days.

I learned from you so many things.
You taught me how to cook.
A great shining example of how to be a loving and giving person.
A wonderful wife and mother!

You loved my girls so very much.
Doting on them with food and love.
Taking pleasure in spending time creating memories that will last a lifetime!

When I remarried and had a son.
You shared in my joy of what God had given to complete my life.
A child who made you smile in your times of trouble and sadness.

But the greatest gift of all was the lessons of faith.
Shown to me the need to live and walk with God each and every day.
A wonderful personification of grace!

Mema, you were the hero of my life.
I miss you so much.
Someday on the other side on heaven's beautiful shores
We will once again be reunited.

Amazing Love

When I think back to yesterdays, I remember the love, kindness,
and compassion I encountered that first day.

You helped me pick up the pieces of my broken heart.
You prayed and encouraged me to take a path to a better start.

You taught me to embrace my faith, and showed me God's grace
Through the struggles I faced each and every day.

You showed me how to forgive like our Heavenly Father above.
Acceptance was mine shown through the eyes of God's unconditional love.

As you grew feeble and old. I counted it all joy to care, my ministry to embrace
The tremendous debt of love that I could never repay.

Pepa, I know you are in Jesus' arms.
The one you served with such commitment and love.
And I know I will see you again when it is time for me to go home.

2010

A Eulogy of Love

For the longest time Heaven was knocking at your door.
Praying and longing for rest. To go and be with the ones who loved you best.
With tears in my eyes, I held your hand wishing you could stay.
But yet I knew it was okay and time for you to go home far away.

Grief exploded in my heart when they called to say that you had passed away.
The Lord took you gently and peacefully in the morning on a hot July day.
You were the only man in my life who truly loved and respected me.
Shown to me what an earthly father's love should really be.

Agape Love, unconditional and free. Never judgmental or condemning.
Always living by example what should be. Examples of Christian living.
A great message of eternal hope. Selfless commitments and ministries.
A living example of the Lord lived so others could believe.

But yet you were so humble often marveling that God had used you,
An imperfect man, to do such mighty and fantastic deeds!
My prayer is to be those wonderful things you instilled in me.
The principal virtues of God's love and grace.
A humble commitment of faith.

Someday on those distant shores when heaven and earth will meet.
The hope of the Lord will bring about a reunion of Love;
A resurrection of great victory!

October 2010

The Heart of Love

COME DANCE WITH ME

I whisper softly, "I'm being reborn."
Take me in your arms and dance with me till the early morn.

Come let us explore, the magic that used to be.
Renew and kindle the spark into a sensual flame.

Come dance with me; I'm still young.
I'm still beautiful inside and out.
"Look at me and want me," I want to shout.

I'm still the one you used to court and danced with till the morning lore.
Come dance with me lest we are torn apart.

2010

Right and Wrong

Help me Lord, to remember what is right and wrong.
These feelings I have are so strong and it has been way too long.
The one I am with says he loves me
but we exist to play a part day by day of tiring
And lifeless commitments held by timeless dull refrains.

I once had a passion that burned brightly,
But through the numerous storms it grows less.
Is it still there; is it dead?
You take it so lightly.

Lord, I am just a woman.
I feel the burning and longing!
Can't he wake up and see what I really need?
Pay attention to me.

2010

Behave

I'm trying to tame what's in my heart.
It's not easy; where do I start?
The one I'm with says to behave—
Yes father I'll obey?
But as I coyly look at him, I say
"You know you'll never make me".

2010

The Story of Tamar

I'm a graceful Palm tree.
My name is Tamar.
A king's daughter who wore colors of royalty of the virgin born.
I was sweet and kind of the purest thought.
Very beautiful and lovely with the purest of heart.

It started with a crush and it grew into such big lust.
A look of undaunted love by a half-brother that I trust.
He took bad advice to feign to be unwell
So that he could have me in private all to himself.

I gladly came to administer and take care,
But he took me by the hand and said,
"Come lie with me in my bed."

Despite my pleas of no folly and doing the right thing
He took what he wanted and then kicked me out with great hate.
I tore my clothes of color and put ashes on my head.
I went to my family in great sorrow and dread.

The rest is in the Bible if you care to see how it ends.
It nearly tore a kingdom apart in four fold sins.

2010

Guardian Angel

Are you my Guardian angel given charge over me,
Singing soft little lullabies meant only for me?
Will you be there in my troubles and the precious moments too,
Smiling at me with eyes so dark, sweet and lovely?
Are you my messenger who will stand up to protect,
With strong arms to lean on when I'm sad and petulant?
Are you an angel camouflaged in shades of light,
A heavenly body to give me joy and delight?
When I think of angels I think of hope that is renewed.
A connection that comes from knowing you.

2010

Awakenings

Since I met you face to face, I feel such desire.
The beauty I feel has begun to emerge.
Your music brings out the passions that I have held deep inside.
Your songs ignite my soul.
What am I to do with this? How do I deal with this craziness?
This makes me feel so strange.
My dreams at night are of great delight.
Fantasies color my daytime hours.
My inner being on fire with desire.
Emotions far exquisite than I have ever felt.
I quiver with great sensual heights that beg release to be set free.
My changes bring to new beginning passions that have been awakened.
Sweet longings that I am living.
Awaken my soul and anticipate the future that brings great promise
Those blossoms flowering passions of such delights.

2010

This is a poem that reflects how I felt when I began to let go of the food addictions that had long held me captive. The highs and lows of emotions I began to experience. It is then that God gave back to me my abilities to write again.

Bittersweet Desire

I can't help it. When I think of you I feel great delight.
My heart is racing and I feel this great desire.
I have this longing down deep in my soul.
This sensuality that makes me feel so unsettled as a whole.

I am working hard to make this earthly vessel
As beautiful as the spirit that occupies,
Which makes up the very essence of my life.

I hope someday that you want me as much as I want you.
Finding me to be most beautiful and complete.
Not just a person to be admired for beautiful qualities on the inside.
But realizing there is much more to be desired.

But until then, I will fantasize and dream of
What I feel and hope will come to be
A bittersweet desire between you and me.

2010

A poem to the one I love!

The Heart of Friendship

FRIENDSHIP

What is Friendship?
What makes the connection?
Is it having that special someone who cares and accepts?
Is it someone you let deep inside?
Someone who shares the real side of life?

Or are you that person who says you have to do this or do that?
Or the one who is willing to ride the exhilarating roller coaster called life?
Are you willing to be part of another pain,
Willing to overlook eccentricities that make one unique,
The oddities that sometimes bring heartache and blame?

So when you think on these things
Ask yourself this question:
Am I worthy to share in this wonderful thing,
A privilege and honor to be called a friend?

2010

The Charmer

Oh dear what am I to do when I think of you.
Are you just a crazy phase?
Do you charm all the ladies this way?
When you smile at me it makes me happy
But then you say things that frustrate and make me insane.
But then you sing such beautiful songs and inspire me to be the best.
And bring out the artist that I thought was long dead.
Now you are ignoring me and making me sad.
I told you I'm sorry but I won't beg you my friend.
I am just a human and sometimes bad,
I'm sorry I frustrated you and made you mad.
So here it is a poem hopefully to make you laugh
And be the charmer I like to joke and share with.

2010

Gentle Plea

Do you know how much you mean to me and how much I care?
I long to be more than just passing friends.
You intrigue me with your abilities and make me strive to be the very best.

In the past you have made me so very happy;
Yet here lately you have made me very sad.
I know I am stubborn in some of my stances.
But life has made me a strong-willed woman.

I know that God has given me the endurance
To fight to be better both physically and in mind,
but sending special people in this life is what it is all about.

I see past the indifference and I know down deep you care.
I keep my distance because of the things I'm walking through,
But it would be nice to have my friend to walk with me too.

I wish I could undo the crazy things in my past.
But please remember I was not fully myself.
Walking through the process of change is not easy and can be a pain.

Acceptance and forgiveness are the basis for relationships be it lover or friend,
The reason that keeps most of humanity living.
Without it there would be no kindness.

A person can strive to seek perfection.
But imperfections are there at every turn.
Passion and love is what makes life worth living, the excitement of another day.

I have a path that deviated from what I wanted to do,
But soon I will find my way and I will get to where I want to be.
It was just a glitch along the way.

I'm trying new things and feel really happy.
My mind and body are healing, but yet there is just this one thing.
So I say with a gentle plea, please let's start over and let it be a better thing.

June 2010

The Heart of Nature

God, the creator of all heaven and earth, thank You, Lord, for all that You have made. The beauty of this magnificent earth. My journey allows me to look around and to admire the handiwork of the Supreme artist. Help me, Lord, to appreciate the beauty of all things around me. Calm my busy heart and soul; teach me to rest in the Universe of Your unending love. Let me always worship the Creator!

Gentle Showers

Looking in the distant hills I see the mists are forming.
The rolling fog and whipping winds announce the lighted darkness.
The coolness of the sprinkles leaves with me exquisite feelings.
I love the wetness on my skin;
I close my eyes and feel the tingling sensations.
My pores breath and come alive with the most sensuous vibrations.

Walking fast in the warm spring showers
Makes my heart race and the laughter that pours out
Is the sound of carefree friends and giddy lovers.
If you were here with me
I would hold your hand and skip along in rhythm
With the flow of the falling rain that strums a steady beat like beautiful music.

Yes, I love the gentleness.
It makes me feel so safe.
Its solace calms my thoughts and brings floods of rest,
A deep meditation of peace.
I pray for the gentle spring showers.
The longing for the cruel dryness to be over.
Bring about refreshing springs from heavens window to end the long drought.

2010

Storms of Life

In the middle of the night I wake up
To hear the awesome crash and the howling winds.
I see the streaking lights brightly zigzagging
And forking out through the tumultuous clouds.

The violent repose echoes through the night.
The sizzle and snap comes from conduit sparks that light up the night sky.
Courting and dancing along in spectacular sight.

The pounding and shaking sends through me
A sigh and shiver as sounds reverberate through the blackest black.
Wild stormy winds break through the trees as they wave in submissive surrender.

Then the downpour; the reward of the animated crescendo.
The opening of heaven's windows to unleash with all its fury
The bounty onto the parched thirsty land.

When all is spent and given, the rain takes a different feat.
A gentleness of a steady stream that lulls me back
Into a contented sleep with interludes of slumbering peace.

In the dawning I wake up to find air so crisp and crystal clear.
The sky radiates with clean refreshing hues of blues
With just a touch of spring in the morning youth.

The wind once more is peaceful.
Forgotten is the gale.
Cool breezes softly blow in tune with the rising sun
That spreads it gentle fingers upon the dampened ground.

The grass and flowers give forth their perfume
Of sweet musky scents of the richest aromas
That teases and tickles the sensational noses of both body and senses.

Like the roses as they unfold, the coolness invades
Their swirling vases popping open delicate scented petals
To share also in the glorious morning affair.

I love the thunderstorms of life.
Not because of their nature, but the aftermath of what they bring
Reap the benefits bringing with it the harvest of newness.

Such things are born and the beauty exposed.
Life experiences are shaped giving birth to a better way
To live more spiritually and sensually with each new day.

2010

Beautiful Spring

The wind is rustling through the trees.
The winter dearth is over.
The frost is gone and the snow has finally melted.
The birds are chirping sweet melodies orchestrating through the breezy meadows.
I thrill to see their antics.
The males with their puffy plumes try hard to impress
The fickle little ladies with their crazy mating dance.

The sprouting buds and luscious vines with their little vases
Will soon burst forth with colorful hues in warm delightful places.
A collage of colors that rivals the spectrum
Will soon blanket the foothills and valleys of this awakening earth.
Yes, spring is finally here.
Bringing with it the season of rebirth
And the warm sunshine of flowering love and hope.

2010

Snapshot of a View

I wish you could see a living snapshot
of an ariel view so beautiful and serene.
A canopy of green lines in my vision of trees up high.
Oh! What a lovely scene.

A horizon of hills that line the sky of historic plains
that tells a story of their own.
Majestically set against skies of turquois blue
With clouds of billowy plumes.

Standing high and looking down, I see the city against the backdrop.
Existing on a different plane are those who scurry back and forth.
Like little ants, so busy with their own thoughts,
Moving in sync as life unfolds to a different beat but yet in the same universal sea.

Thinking back to long ago,
I wonder what there must have been before progress brought
All these things of inventions human kind has come to understand.

Imagination brings to mind the Indians and the buffalo that graced the land.
Of soldiers and pioneers who braved the wild
And forged a living by their own hands.

These romantic things exist in my thoughts and dreams.
Where hardships forged our freedoms and our sacred beliefs.
A snapshot of the past that meets future and present things.

2010

Soaring Free

Up in the skies of blue seas
I see a beautiful bird of Supreme Being.
Floating aloft so free, soaring on wind and wings
Oh how I wish that was me!
In my dreams I reach great heights of joy,
But on earth I'm captured in this daily flurry.
But someday I can let go of this earthly realm
And let my fetters be unbound.
Let me soar on wings to a better spirit.
Shedding all that is holding me from soaring
To places I know I can be.
To places I can fly free.
The clouds and sun beckon me with their splendor of the air.
The free-fall of the open spaces thrills me
As I take off to whimsical flights of time.
I open up my arms to coast like the birds in the sky.
And swoop down to observe the geographical patterns
Of this sweet earth drawn into the land.
My soul and spirit climb up to the rugged peaks of the mountaintops.
Where eagles rise up on majestic wings
And soar up to the expanse of the heavens.
Then sadly I must come back down
To this sodden place to alight in the valleys.
To awake to find I am bound to such realities of time once again.
But you see I am a dreamer.
I close my eyes and see that I can be anything I please.
Having the freedom to live out all my earthly dreams.

2010

Edwards Brothers, Inc.
Thorofare, NJ USA
May 4, 2011